The Messier Objects

Michael Zand

The Messier Objects

Shearsman Books

First published in the United Kingdom in 2015 by
Shearsman Books
50 Westons Hill Drive
Emersons Green
BRISTOL
BS16 7DF

Shearsman Books Ltd Registered Office
30–31 St. James Place, Mangotsfield, Bristol BS16 9JB
(this address not for correspondence)

www.shearsman.com

ISBN 978-1-84861-456-7

ACKNOWLEDGEMENTS
Special thanks to Alex Davies, Stephen Emmerson, Steven Fowler,
Alan Hay, Jeff Hilson, Peter Jaeger, Keith Jebb, SL Mendoza, and
David Miller for their interest and support.

Many thanks also to my family for their encouragement and patience:
it's not easy living with a stargazing poet.

for Carrie

Foreword

A few words on the title and theme of the collection. The Messier Objects are a catalogue of astronomical bodies discovered and published by Charles Messier in 1771. Messier was a comet hunter and was frustrated by seeing objects in the sky that he thought were comets, but turned out to be random and uninteresting clouds of dust. He drew up the list to avoid comet hunters wasting time on what he regarded as the "worthless detritus of the skies". Ironically it was later discovered that these objects were in fact galaxies, nebulae and other deep sky phenomena, and in fact Messier is now better known for his hated "detritus" than for his comet hunting.

The Messier Objects uses these astronomical entities as a starting point, or more precisely, a point of extrapolation. At one level they are a fairly disparate and occasionally playful set of musings. At a deeper level they are my meditations on the colour and complexity of the universe, and a rejection of the drift that we are seeing all around the world to cultural polarisation, simplification and standardisation. Hence it is also a play on the Messier being "messier" objects, and there is a political subtext to all this too of course. There are within the collection the ghosts of a number of figures who have fought for their vision of a pluralistic and tolerant world. I will not name the figures here – frankly I don't think it matters if you do not recognise them. The key thing is that they are in there, giving resonance and purpose to *The Messier Objects* through their own words and actions.

Those of you familiar with my work will know that it is rarely easy to decipher in terms of meaning or narrative, and *The Messier Objects* is no exception. I would urge you, as I always do, to worry less about the meanings and more about the impact of the sounds, forms and rhythms of the poems. Sometimes this approach will take you into random, unexpected and seemingly irrelevant places, but as with Messier's objects themselves, these places can be extraordinary and deeply powerful.

Michael Zand
Istanbul, 19th June, 2015

M1

is vaguely in the shape of an apple tree

how much time do you have
these star clouds are all that's left

anything you say
anything with a word in it
has been exhausted

you see they think up games
yarns that hang over us
like a false regression or
a chance to regress or
books with too many book marks

yet between their stitches and their hard drives
is a thin plectrum that plays a hollow mono sound

these star clouds are all that's left
they are our horses
it's the sky or the wine and the sky that makes us –

M2

like all geeks
he had a one-track mind

sounds harsh
and it is
it's meant to be

at times he studied the cracks
the cracks within the cracks
he developed his own hinterlands of despair

he knew the value of new words too
the fact that pencils breed pens
that pencils are in way just like pens
but a bit less hard

and in the close-up
just off kilter from the main bands of spectral light
he would avert his vision

and see a poet's heart or a —

M3

a panoramic view
a motion less in the torrid
not an ocean of angry points

or at least not now

the face of –

M4

he's all surfaces

he may terrify us with his wondrous crown of lies
but he's not and never will be
merely beautiful

worry beads in effect tell us that he's –

M5

i want you
to agree to
do something

i know of
two priests
who will set
off in the same
direction as you
soon or very
soon or now

i want you
to consider
joining them
but if you do
stay with them
close to them
until they –

The Butterfly Cluster

this is where our first names came from
carried to us through the universe
embedded in rock and ice so that we could –

M7

he was a good-looking young man, probably about
the same age as her

tall
and slim and fair

he wasn't married and they got on just fine
but they didn't exchange addresses because they felt it a
little false a little tempting of fate

he gave her a talisman which she treasured

she gripped it tight when they –

The Lagoon Nebula

this is the temple
this is where she was killed as if in a garden
her imagination and ours run through it
we were built of this

sounds and chants
from the red and infra-red ends of the spectrum
and all the sweeter for it brother

and she remains here in the –

M9

Dangerfield, Daniel, Danzig, Daphne, Dardenelle,
Dar-es-Salaam, Dariush, Darayavoosh, Dasht-e-Lut,
Darwin, Dante, David, Davood, Dearborn, Decopolis,
Deneb, Denebs, Dachau, Death.

Noor-un-Nisa Inayat, Noora, Noor, Madeleine, Marie,
Maria, Maria-Nisa, Jeanne-Marie.

She was and is our —

M10

For ten months, she was kept there shackled, at her hands and feet. Scratching on coffee cups, the names of her favourite herbs and herbal teas.

There are no excuses for the actions of men against the stars.

At least we have these few bright specks and smudges, my sister.

Stars shift above us. A little at a time. Year after year. Their patterns change, until they are forgotten, or —

The Wild Duck Cluster

spring and summer
autumn

succeeds with a pulse or beat

like an immense religious love it makes us –

The Herculean Cluster

i've killed too many brain cells
these past few years trying to understand
their need for monosynthesis

when you dig
you get dirt
on your hands and fingers

this is what they call the hurts
and they hate it
because it makes us strong
because it makes us us
it makes us –

M14

there's something in the music of this place
and also within me
ticking

like a
pilgrimage

it —

The Wild Duck Cluster

there are only really three poems
they just flap about a lot
in different guises

a garden
a garden rose and

a man or a woman on a bed dreaming of –

M15

i'm not a honey bee
gone at first sight of smoke
or a cheeky banshee
who leaves when there's trouble

or a historian of peacocks
taking care of my own
broken like a swollen flood
bleeding out on a river bed

like a casual friend saying —

M16

which makes me wander
whether under this
dream

there are
streams with
rafts of words
that you hear
with your eyes
like the buzz
of branches
in the wind
and the owls
breathing hard
as if to say
it's ok to be here
to dream this

a gentle disruption of –

The Horseshoe Nebula

casting a line
our wishes
in the seas
of santiago
our minds
are porous
a bloody mess
remembering colour
a supernova of hurts
amanda and manuela
the remnants shimmer here

songs were a series of boats carrying his body to the —

M18

after a while we discover we are in a kind of hell

then we
realise
this abyss
however deep
is the end
of something

special
like a
whole way of life

or like a stone with a hole in it
or the palms of his broken bloodied hands in a –

M19

this alternative to place is

forced on us
to be quiet
to live quietly

a stadium of death once stood here which

makes me
reject it
like blood
on concrete
roses burn too

saplings still
muscle through
like young football
they create beauty
under cover of
even here
even after the –

M20

hands
there were words before hands
before songs for manuela
before the hurts
before

lead us from this place

lead us from dark to a manifest
filling up of hearts
for our world, our universe
our peace with –

M21

sit with me . here on
the ledge in abundance
as the winter groundswell rolls
under us and then under us

you . with red raw palms
both of us . gripping the flag tight
and the lord dancing and digging in
for any bird that swoops and dies

will leave this place . to the spectral rats
or the giant donkeys of the shitty centre
but purples remain . as do the lanterns
paper and fire . persist and subsist by —

brothers sisters in sanctuary
in a shout of virtue or praise or
good will . we remain

as the revenants of —

The Sagittarius Cluster

On the morning of September 12, he was taken away by the military, along with thousands of others deemed suspect, and interned as a prisoner in a football stadium.

He was tortured, electrocuted and had his wrists and hands broken. His hands were seen as a symbol of his craft as a poet and songwriter.

On September 16, he was machine-gunned to death.

M23

The Sagittarius Star Cloud

M25

there was once a leaf
with veins . strands
with each other . de coeur
it danced . turned
was . as ore . lit up
in and out . of the sun
it blotted the earth
as it skipped
catching a drop or two
skirting . in . this
place spits . and slits
honest . worthy . de coeur
from an unknown tree
and at the end . when it fell
there were new roots
from the stretch . the sky
breaking the earth and –

M26

dawn here is
like a jaeger marrakesh
slowly etching us with lotus

stealing a scythe or a great bell
burning away the salt
we try again
to colour in this place

ending our –

The Dumbbell Nebula

fire place

in side as one piece
covered in plaster is dead
hungered with the weave
these tools are not enough

knuckling away

led by chisels of metal
cracked and cowed
a new stellar peace
and in its heart

enough to –

M28

stuck in a rush

amongst the cinders
the archaeology of amiri baraka
in a voiceless life and times is
an archive of uncertainty
sanity kneels on words

briefly it move us   un settle us

breathes bereaves

but –

M29

for a few francs we
buy warmth we
network socially we
mind the gap

the draughtmanship of respectability
even though we hate these smudges
of the skies or
is the genius of our own—

M30

they are coming
slowly at us
these stars
these horses

lord knows
when it will end

but when it does
we'll seem primitive to –

The Andromeda Galaxy

if i could live
this life again
without fame
i would
i would be
young anxious
without Prozac
the ultimate
happiness
machine
am i too old
for a jumpsuit
or my friend
john's brown
cardigan or a
book of desserts
with the spine
removed of —

M32

in this nasty little battle
for the ultimate
luxury
hotel
spa

we
sigh
sharing
toiletries
exchanging words
as if they were meant to –

Triangulum

if i could live
this life again
without fame
i would
i would be
young and anxious too
like the mother
of all perspirations
of all comebacks
of all comb-backs

after a while
i'd go dutch
enjoy my
spectacles again
with such
vigour vigour
that all the
poetry in the
world would seem
tired like
showers draped
against all the –

M34

these star clusters are like organ music
an anger pervades them

the terrace of a noodle bar
after good poetry or bad prose
has the stench of leonard cohen

a shadow in the –

M35

nostalgia tea
is like good soul music

we steal a few boarts
like hornworts
spellbound

by the travails
of our cups
our sachets of sucrose
our long lost beats
our

zing zing zing is a —

M36

poetry lacks a little
safety
sometimes it has too much
safety

like a guru
it wants us to –

M37

we waved good-bye to an astronaut
like dick van dyke in mary poppins
or the bloke who does the ads for xfm

or the effigy of a penis

we hear little from him these days
or from his herbs and spices
the turmeric which once fired us

we carry on regardless
we pretend it's OK to pre-judge
to consign him to the past
but it's not

it makes a mockery of the –

M38

is the dark thickset young man with piercing eyes who –

M39

blue
pink
blue
roses
cubes
circles

violence

birds
the dreams of birds of –

The Winnecke Four

anyone that carries
more than five books
at a dinner party is
an enemy of the people

which is rubbish of course
and by the way the
obscure corners
of any dinner party are
a poverty of words
and bad coffee
and machines that fail
even by their own
sad standards to produce
difference and difficulty

and in our pursuits
of the beats
and rhythms
we stay well-read
in a world of four –

M41

is in a world
where the central figure is a

multiple limbed interpreter

each limb a memory of –

Orion

London
Kinshasa
Vegas
Saigon
Inside
Outside
Windows
Traces
Gorses
Chasms narrow
A quagmire of signs
Sometimes blood on the city streets

Lisbon
Kazan
Riyadh
Rome
Inside
Outside
Old dust
Concrete
Fountains
Tongues on ice
A life of black gloves
They left them red by rivers and forests

Lusaka
Louisville
Athens
Lips
Inside
Outside
Nodding
Humming to
Beats from the
Ashik and music
Across the hinterland
Your verses sub versed in an effort to be a –

M43

new york city
was like this once was

filthy and incurable in its own –

The Beehive Cluster

in the company of invalids beggars
pitiful resigned outcasts
hopeless victims of an implacable fate
hopeful victims of placable fate
artists of anxiety
artists of disgust
artists of the human excrement
everything exterior that is landscapes flowers fruit

the eight colour of the solar spectrum is a —

The Pleiades

he slobbers as the dead do
counting his money
counting the thirsty ones
grinning masks
in caramel in difference
one place at a time
the chickens are coming
like millionaire shortbreads
blackened in blacktitude

is a gang of champs is
lagers rising
man on the floor with a
no body is no body
snatch me a sweet dark kiss
a long trip to ahab
elmo is king of the fat ones

recoil redeem redeem
bristling too in blacktitude
sorcering with a bus
dogs operate his sirens
don't mess with them
don't tip them either
but watch stay close to

muriel of the murinals
queen of the cider press
is bald and bellied
with a right hand lens
a man in the rigging
at the gate of a farm
chicken is plucked and fat
chicken is ready for the –

M46

i / he / we

become an
emperor of the moon
gypsy in a world of –

M47

when we
stop for a while and drink
along the mississippi delta
take a sip

dream
of ever faster speeds and streams

in a place where there are many windows
some low and some covered in –

M48

the sea

or part of it
un due waves
crystals

you won't find it here
or anywhere

on the waves
they make a multiplicity of tiny –

M49

I am the greatest you've got.
I am the part you won't recognize. But get used to me.

I am black and red and green, confident and cocky.
<u>My</u> name is Ahab, not yours. It always was.

<u>My</u> religion is the lyric, not yours.
<u>My</u> goals are the grasses and the birds; you are the other.

What you're thinking, right now, is all that you'll be.
I am the greatest you –

M50

bumble bee jazz
has never appealed to us

even in our seventies
we preferred daf

to sax and the many many —

The Whirlpool Galaxy

come . like enthusisasts come
on a shuttle . leaping for a train
hurtling through an eye of a cat
a circular blaze of fireworks . or
come . as you are . and we'll eat fish
you'll see . everything changes
and when the irish say . bend it
like beckham . in the o zone
we'll pay extra for the lotto
and watch them burn in the starlight
like doozies . like constructs
and we'll dine on a pig's back . po-faced
poe . come on . give us more than ham
je vous demande un peu . monsieur poe
again and again . onwards . upwards
poe . ham . away with the farm
is an excuse . a worry . a syndicate
stitch it . stretch it . make it tingle
come . roll in a spectrum of greyscale
a painted upper lip . is bitten . stiffens to –

W

am tired of advocates
and of them . actually
i don't hate them . no
quite the opposite
it's quite beyond them
like a sphere or a suffix
of praxis . of schism
to explain the absence
of soldiers . law courts
waged on women or
attendants of life or
lions and lionesses

am tired of the sweep
run them in circles . scatter
but never let them go
never let them deepen
grip hold of each fibre
like forough or emmeline
like the ghost of noor
like the priests of the sun
the sea flags are aligned
blowing in the gusts
blowing for the gusts

for us as an i or a we
and i . we urge you
you . as a man or men
to be difficult . complex
a grievence propellor
not colour me by numbers or

make me glitter . the them
are deaf . deaf . deaf . de
to a choice of each evil

please forgive these
living breathing breasts or
brutal question marks
with a baby that cries or
an end . end less politics
papers soaked in snow
from the beginning it is
as she smiles for us both
of a cat and a mouse
for the future . for the fight
to help wither this –

M53

red wine or the memory of –

M54

they were never really there
red wine or white wine

they never openned
there was no bearded man with a carrier bag
no cheap books and zines
no fan base

no steve or steve or steve
no jeff

just a sequence of uncomfortable plastic chairs that we –

M55

From all the Circles
Came war on the horizon
Birds swooped from the water
Snatching away carcasses
Making the lion lose his tongue
Making us bloodied like an ajam
Tongueless in a new world
Outside on the inside

We or our ancesters
Kept an inner Soul by which we lived and died
In the tradition of us
Like the hands of Jara
LIKE THE SEMBLANCE OF A MOUSE
Clinging to a broken road

We or our ancesters
Were crimson with rubies
The gems of those seeking righteousness, and the
        displacement of righteousness
Tongueless in a new world
Inside on the outside

But I wasn't there
I may be too old for the Bloodaxe
But I'm not an old enough to remember
Perhaps the lion never died
Lives on in the stars
To appease our children and our Teachers and our
        Documentary Makers

Anyway, the birds moved on
Smoke seeping from their veins
In search of the mystic cure
The cunning panacea of the mind
Through yearning, love, gnosis and bejazzlement
Through unity, madness, selflessness and oblivion

To dive into in to a shallow grave
Neither Frasier nor Forman
Neither Chica nor Limona
Neither Aslan nor Assad
A memory of the spring purple
Wounded by the trees

But we still stand here

Like the say, "from cloud comes fish"
The road's still broken, still ours
Fair thee well
LIKE THE SEMBLANCE OF A MOUSE
Tongueless in a new world
Outside on the inside as though we're all –

Lyra

the methods
of our society
are cheap shots
murder breeds murder
in the eastern sky

but in the trees
live conferences of birds
who aspire to sing
even when they were herded in pens
made no more than bones

they move like sparrows
how sparrows move just before –

M57

rain drops
sink into these stitches like a —

M58

the daughters of scars, fights
healing the hurt of others
a little

let them

make us an emblem for persistence
humble and
against an openly troubled sea
piano and strings and –

M59

by the sand breaks
sun loaded down

an old man drifts
teased to sleep
i told you so

arab stories
keep us –

M60

love gems
love cushions, red
love cushions, black
an "i love you" canvas
i love curls too, professional curls
circle of love so sweet, figurine
circle of love is the future, figurine
circle of love my family, my life, my love, figurine

home is made of love and dreams, canvas
truth in sterling silver, lucky in love in gold
edmund hardy "ladies love love us & kill us" body bar
tiny love wonder wheel
love letters block
love in the –

M61

Like palm trees, they are series of visual and tactile images that reflect our affirmative if also anguished thirst for –

M62

the horses many times they
to narrow the chasms brother
the quagmire of our signs
drink mey
in tehran or tel aviv

kiss hands lips

again we —

The Sunflower Galaxy

habibi my little one or azizam too
you are my universe
little lion with a sword
on a green and flag

on a
on a
on
a
a

aaaaaaaaaaaa —

M66

i speak out t t
from nahaayat
nahaayat . t. t

infin . at . depth . in the night
n . high . yet
for this is what we have come

and you come to see at my house
as a friend
or in the spirit of a friend
bring in a lamp and a window to
look .
at the crowds in the happy city streets

they peak by . a . a
as if to
nahaayat . . t

M67

here near the house
in this tiny un night
the wind caresses
branches
listen to it
it whispers us
cherishes us
to the point of hap
it panes and fraps
the window the —

green clean green
this late ray of the sun
not found in books
or family trees
it makes us smile
palms against the glass
for a moment it or we
are the universe
in the wind
as we are
will be
it carries us
it carries to —

Hydra

horses
spark fire
in a cloud of dust
a little too much blood

they see us here
flawed by —

M69

dichten is to cut
a human invention

like the bloods
dante liked noise

given good books
par boiled . revealed

in a sense active
always moving us

texts are turned
by the margins by us

but like khan younis
the end is never so —

M70

I must speak.

Today, I'm covered with nettles and branches. The grass that's stretches over me – here – is not so easy – neither for the ants nor the leaves. I am witness to the trees that once grew here. It is not so easy – as there are blood-stained stones on each side of this road, each side of me, each with their own shadow. It is certainly not so easy for the cats, or the families of the cats, who eat roses or threaten to eat them at least, now they know I'm buried and locked in by these branches. And it is not so easy for the many thousands who grew the roses in their many colours, and sacrificed them, one after another, in a long strong bleed of red, surrounded by broken towers and broken promises. Must speak. Today, I'm covered with nettles and branches. My words, brothers and sisters, are almost forgotten. In the midst of this hellish jungle, my carcass festers. But I still flinch and twitch. I still offer a memory of a slow summer day in Galilee, where we played together as children and watched oranges grow on our modest orange trees. Must speak. Yet they, the propellers of hate, offer nothing in return, not even some daytime moonlight. As I pull these thickets from my worm-addled torso, there is still the black of the rock and the grunt of the axe. There is still the grunt of the shine of the axe and all its constituent parts. But in this deathscape, something sundered still persists. By scene, by sentence, something is rendered back.

I must speak.

Let me say to you, the sun and the moon: my body is still young.
Even in death it comes engraved with energy and obduracy. A
line or a phrase of love runs down the side of my face like a half
forgotten morning call. I say to you, my friends, I'm covered
with nettles and branches. I say in a loud and a clear –

M71

Today, I'm a ghost.

The signing of these Principles, here by the Roses, was not so easy. Not easy for the families of the victims of the wars, the violence, the terror, whose pain will never heal. Not easy for the many thousands who have defended these roses, and even sacrificed their lives for them. Today, I am a ghost. But I'm not a saint or a martyr. I was born to break bones and broke many bones. I have come from Jerusalem, as you come from Jerusalem. We have come from peoples, homes, families that have not known a single year, not a single month in which mothers have not wept for their sons.

We have come to try and put an end, again, to the age of sacrifice so that our children, our children's children, will no longer experience the unspeakable pain of its silent emptiness. Let me say to you: we are destined to live together in a less empty land. I and you have returned from battle stained with blood. I and you have seen friends and enemies killed before our eyes. I and you have attended funerals and could not look into the eyes of their parents. I and you, but especially you, come from a land where parents bury their children, with thorns scratched across their children's palms.

Today, I am a ghost, and I say to you in a loud and a clear voice: Muspeek. Enough. Enough of blood and tears. Enough. I and you, but especially you, are people with soil and dust on our hands. And with these hands we can break the earth between us, to love, to live side by side in dignity, in empathy, as human beings, as free peoples.

Today, I'm a ghost.

And I still tear through, for the sake of these roses, for the love
of these roses, and say again to you: Enough. Enough. Enough.
Let us pray that one day a day will come when we all will say —

M72

is against ignorance and generals
and the life of gloves

we are its —

M73

They create distorted realities with lights and colours that go beyond logic and concept to engender and convey the –

M74

those who read
against the grain
get good deals
big components
epics imitations
to break up the
benidorms singing
both what it is and
when it gets far –

M74

The "form of its escape" refers to the illusion that we can
actually see the path of a rapidly fleeing we object.
If we could, we would —

M75

a longish dull
stretch
shortly after
the carriages
have fallen off

aimlessly a way
make us feel
popular . like all
cheap things

we've destroyed enough for one –

M76

I could easily connect it with the writing of Imagist poems, or with Apollinaire or Cummings. But I won't. These star clouds are stars in their own right. Individual clouds of gases and molecules and —

M77

a tight mesh holds us
holds the good
to the less good
different climates
different bloods
intermittent grunts
forough at the window
noor in her field
cassius holding a book
yitzak as a ghost
and victor with his palms to the sky

we plunder them sometimes love them
like dry tannin in the throat
we make the effort to live again

as we drift in to the heart of –

M78

It takes a particular human experience to freeze the meaning of form, of the substances and forces of our universe, and extend the warmth of this place to our uni verse or –

M79

this great break
is an inflection
wagging tails
doing nothing

making brutes of us
losing balance . its
a whole art poised

like Beowulf
we are circles and colours
we drink beer warm
to the interpretations of –

M80

it doesn't matter
which leg you
four legs stand and
in the long they

rice paper poets
were asylum seekers
deferences of what

idioms and idiots
all finished here in the –

Johan Elert Bode

This is impossible to light or to smoke as it exudes the –

The Cigar Galaxy

anyone that carries
more than five books when
they visit a hospital is

which is also full
by the way
of obscure corners
a poverty of words
and bad coffee
and machines that fail
even by their own
modest standards are

and in our pursuits
of the beats
and rhythms
of a well read life
or a well read —

M83

fig and parsley and drift wood
percussions revolve around the –

M84

Yet others see this is a playful melody, regard it as an affectionate portrait. There is said to be love in my delivery, which many believe overrides any confusion aroused by the neediness of my lyrics. If that's true, this is as close as I will ever get to a thank you or an apology. And even then I –

M85

and afterwards
we climb
above the town
to the rocks
where we once

and watch the rush
the pebble dance
and divide
below us as it

comes and –

M86

You've had your fun, they'll soon imply. You're intruding now, an over-burdened middleman. You're impossibly balanced on your many left legs. You're squat, dour and frenzied, with a rubbing cloth attached to your resting hand and –

M87

is a superstar of the urban classses
making us sing for our pennies
vous êtes son people
a capitalist cash dance
his names is toes is
in turns and in spirals
he is a room of falseness

false colour
false taste false sound

false sense of –

M88

a is alef
b is beth
we share these
so let us share these

pey is p
peace is in piece is is
just not with it . these steps

sher is a poem
pey is also pain

peace in is pieces is
not just steps . but also steps

pey is a patronising array of noises but

piece can only by piece by peace
just steps . no . these with it

until k is for kuf . so that

in its many colours
peace is in each piece

and our steps are just —

M89

they seems impossible . these stars
but they are part of us . and remains so beautiful

even though it messes things up
who cares . let them

they are our horses they –

M90

in time england
is narrowing
the world even
a gulf between
the loose leaf clusters and
a dozen small novels
a line at a time   fine

perhaps we can catch it
this slide in curiosity
in register
this popular silence

looking up
we see so many colours
so much happiness
beyond the main sequences
of the regular stars

we're all mad bad and sad
objects of the universe
and in time we'll all —

The Messier Objects

Michael Mehrdad Zand Ahanchian is a writer, editor and researcher. He was born in Iran, but has spent most of his life in London, where he is now Visiting Lecturer in Creative Writing at the University of Roehampton. His research interests lie in alternative translations of Middle Eastern poetry, the use of psychogeography in contemporary literature, and modern readings of the medieval notion of the "Ashik" or wandering poet. His collections include *Kval* (Arthur Shilling, 2009) and *Lion: The Iran Poems* (Shearsman Books, 2010), *The Wire and Other Poems* (Shearsman, 2012) and *Little Rubies* (Three Rivers, 2013). His work was showcased by *Rattapallax* magazine in 2014, which identified him as in the vanguard of the new wave of Internationalism in British poetry. He was included in the *Best Poetry of 2011* anthology (Salt Publishing, 2011) and won the Roehampton Poetry Performance Prize in 2008. Michael has participated in various collaborations with musicians and multi-media artists and read at a wide range of poetry events across Europe. Other projects include an ongoing international translation project called *Lexico*. He is currently working on a contemporary translation of *The Rubaiyat of Omar Khayyam* entitled *Ruby*. In February 2013 his sequence of poems entitled 'Pang' was included in an exhibition on *Poets of the Thames* at the Museum of English Rural Life in Reading, Berkshire.